ERIC HENTY

The Nomadic Professional

How to Work on a Laptop While Seeing the World

This book is dedicated to my wife and son.
They are the fabric of my life and I am so grateful
to both of them for enriching my life. Without their
love and support, I would not be able to accomplish anything
of value in my life, including this book.

And to all
of the digital nomads whose bravery to live a life
on their terms is inspiring to others.

Contents

Preface

"They told me to grow roots, instead I grew wings." – *Louis de Bernières, British Author*

This book is meant to be a guide for all of those brave souls who want to go to other parts of the world for adventure and work, all at the same time.

I have enjoyed learning about how to become a digital entrepreneur myself. I am running a YouTube channel with a friend about art, and another about health and fitness. I am sure that I will create an online course in my future. As an educator, I plan to never stop learning. It keeps me young and interested in the world. If I was younger, I may have considered becoming a digital nomad. It is not an option for me at this stage of my life, however, I have worked overseas and can say that it was a very valuable life experience.

This is why I have written this book. It is a guide for those who are considering packing their bags and working from a laptop while traveling. Embarking on the journey of becoming digital nomad can seem both exhilarating and daunting. The allure of exploring new cultures, experiencing diverse environments, and breaking free from the conventional office space has attracted a growing number of individuals to this lifestyle.

However, the path to success as a digital nomad is not without its challenges. Balancing work and travel, maintaining a steady income, and ensuring personal well-being require a mix of strategic planning, flexibility, and continuous learning.

This book serves as a comprehensive guide to help you navigate the intricacies of the digital nomad lifestyle. Whether you're just starting or looking to refine your approach, the insights and practical advice provided herein are designed to equip you with the tools and confidence needed to thrive. From financial management and productivity tips to health and wellness strategies, each chapter is crafted to support you in building a sustainable and fulfilling life on the road.

As you turn the pages, you'll discover that being a successful digital nomad is not only about remote work but also about creating a harmonious balance between your professional and personal aspirations. With a keen focus on self-care, adaptability, and continuous growth, this book will inspire and empower you to embrace the endless possibilities that come with being a digital nomad. Welcome to your new adventure.

I

Part One

This is the main part of the book, starting with Chapter One (Starting with a Dream) to the Conclusion. Part Two contains the Worksheet suggestions that will help you plan out your journey as a digital nomad and entrepreneur. All great dreams require planning and goals to become a reality. I hope you enjoy the entire read and find it valuable on a journey that is extremely satisfying! God-Speed!

1

Start with a Dream

Everyone who has dreamed of becoming a digital nomad begins to have some type of image in their mind of what they hope to experience. Though the following account is entirely fictional, it could easily be one person's hopes of how becoming a digital nomad would turn out or just as well one person's actual experience. In all actuality, this account is close to a digital nomad's actual story. They even met a woman who became their wife in their travels! You may see yourself in the following account:

My Journey to Becoming a Digital Nomad

Relocating to a beachfront location had always been a dream of mine. The idea of living somewhere that combined my love for the ocean with the flexibility of remote work was too enticing to resist. It all started when I stumbled upon a job listing for a digital marketing position that allowed for 100% remote work. After a few rounds of interviews and a bit of nail-biting suspense, I received the offer.

I packed my essentials, bid farewell to my urban apartment, and embarked on a journey to my new coastal home. Upon arrival, I was greeted by the serene sound of waves crashing against the shore and the warm caress of the sea breeze on my face. Setting up my workspace with a view of the ocean made every task feel less like work and more like a pleasurable activity.

One of the most delightful aspects of my relocation was the opportunity to interact with the local community. The residents were incredibly welcoming, eager to share tips on the best spots to eat, surf, and explore. I quickly became a regular at a quaint beachside coffee shop, where the aroma of freshly brewed coffee mingled with the salty sea air. The staff knew my order by heart – a strong espresso to kickstart my mornings and a refreshing iced coffee for those balmy afternoons.

The beach environment itself was nothing short of magical. My daily routine included early morning walks along the shore, where the soft sand and the lapping waves provided a peaceful start to the day. During breaks from work, I'd often take a dip in the sparkling waters or simply relax under the shade of a palm tree with a good book.

Living and working in a beachfront paradise turned out to be everything I had hoped for and more. The combination of fulfilling work, vibrant community, and stunning natural beauty created a life that felt balanced and enriched. My digital nomad journey was a testament to the incredible opportunities that modern technology can offer, allowing me to blend pro-fessional aspirations with personal passions in a harmonious and invigorating way.

As I continued to explore the local area, I discovered hidden gems and unique experiences that added even more depth to my stay. From snorkeling in crystal clear waters to hiking through lush rainforests, there was always something new and exciting waiting just beyond my doorstep.

But it wasn't just about the exotic adventures or picturesque landscapes – it was also about the culture and connection I formed with the people of this coastal community. From fellow digital nomads to friendly locals, I was welcomed with open arms and felt a sense of belonging that I had never experienced before.

In addition to the fulfilling lifestyle, working remotely also provided me with valuable skills such as time management, adaptability, and effective communication. These are qualities that have continued to benefit me in my professional and personal endeavors long after I left the beach.

But perhaps the most valuable lesson I learned from my time as a digital nomad was the importance of living in the moment and embracing new experiences. It's easy to get caught up in the hustle and bustle of daily life, but taking a step back and immersing yourself in different cultures and surroundings can bring a whole new perspective and appreciation for life.

As I reflect on my digital nomad journey, I am grateful for the memories, lessons, and friendships that I made along the way. It was an experience that shaped me in more ways than I could have ever imagined and one that I will always cherish. So to anyone considering embarking on their own digital nomad journey, I say go for it – the world is waiting to be explored and you never know what amazing opportunities and experiences await you. So pack your laptop, grab your passport, and get ready for the adventure of a lifetime.

Writing out your expectations of what type of digital nomadic experiences you would like to have is an exercise that is recommended. After doing this, the topics and subjects covered in this guide might have a lot more meaning to you. This type of visualization may go a long way in actually helping you prepare for your digital nomadic experience.

2

The Rise of Nomadic Professionals

As the landscape of work continues to evolve, more professionals are discovering the allure of breaking free from the traditional office environment. The concept of the nomadic professional goes beyond just the flexibility to work from home—it embodies the freedom to earn a living while experiencing different cultures, landscapes, and lifestyles. This lifestyle is fueled by the digital revolution, allowing for a seamless blend of work and travel. Gone are the days when a 9-5 job tied individuals to a single location; today, the world can be your office.

The rise of the digital nomad movement is a testament to this shift, where professionals leverage technology to maintain productive careers irrespective of their geographical location. Be it a beach in Bali or a café in Paris, the nomadic professional is characterized by the ability to find a work-life balance that suits their personal goals and aspirations while maintaining their professional responsibilities. This book aims to guide you through the ins and outs of embracing such a lifestyle, from setting up your mobile office to navigating different cultural landscapes, ensuring you thrive both personally and professionally. Welcome to the future of work—one where the world is truly your oyster.

What It Means to Be a Nomadic Professional

Being a nomadic professional means more than just working remotely; it encapsulates a philosophy of living that prioritizes freedom, adaptability, and continuous growth. As a nomadic professional, you unite the realms of work and travel, seamlessly integrating both into a lifestyle that fulfills your wanderlust while sustaining your career. This approach to work allows for unparalleled flexibility, enabling you to set your own schedule and choose your working environment based on your preferences or even your mood.

It's important to understand the different types of digital nomads. Some individuals fully embrace a location-independent lifestyle, traveling from place to place without a permanent home base. Others may prefer a semi-nomadic approach, dividing their time between a few select destinations throughout the year. Understanding where you fit on this spectrum can help you plan your journey more effectively.

Another critical aspect is the variety of professions that lend themselves to this lifestyle. Freelancers, remote employees, entrepreneurs, and even some traditional job roles can be adapted to a location-independent format. The gig economy has also expanded the possibilities, allowing people to engage in short-term contracts or project-based work that can be done from anywhere.

It involves mastering the art of balancing productivity with the spontaneity of travel, ensuring that neither your professional nor personal adventures suffer. The nomadic professional embraces technology and innovation to stay connected and efficient, leveraging tools that facilitate collaboration and communication across distances. Ultimately, being a nomadic professional is about creating a life that is rich with diverse experiences and opportunities, allowing you to explore the world without compromising your career ambitions.

Why the Traditional 9-5 Work Model is Becoming Outdated

The traditional 9-5 work model is increasingly viewed as outdated in today's dynamic and interconnected world. With advances in technology and changes in workforce expectations, the rigid structure of a set hourly schedule is often seen as a constraint rather than a necessity. Many professionals now seek a better work-life balance, which the 9-5 model seldom provides. It doesn't accommodate the diverse needs and lifestyles of the modern worker, who might benefit from more flexible hours to deal with personal commitments, varied peak productivity times, or simply the desire for a more fulfilling life.

Furthermore, the rise of remote work has demonstrated that productivity does not depend on being tethered to a specific location or clocking in at a certain time. Companies that adopt flexible work schedules often notice increased employee satisfaction and retention, alongside improved overall performance. In this evolving landscape, the ability to work asynchronously, collaborate digital platforms, and focus on outcomes rather than hours worked is paving the way for a more progressive approach to professional life.

As the traditional 9-5 work model becomes less relevant, a new wave of professionals is emerging – the nomadic professional. These are individuals who have embraced technology and global connectivity to break free from geographical constraints and traditional office settings. They prioritize their personal growth, experiences, and autonomy over conventional career paths.

The emerging workforce is more apt to examine their options before entering the workforce, as well as professionals who are reassessing their career choices. People have heard Steve Jobs last thoughts before passing away, when he stated that he regretted working so much at the expense of spending more time with loved ones. The COVID pandemic gave people a lot to think about their choices, with people opting to work from home whenever possible. Then, there are the entrepreneurs who have decided to embrace a new way of working, away from brick and mortar establishments. They have chosen to take the risks and rewards of working for themselves for a variety of reasons, whether it be more time with family or the ability to adjust their own work schedules. This book is devoted to those who want to live a nomadic lifestyle so that they can work and travel at the same time.

Some people begin in a professional role while staying in one established residence and begin to add travel to their itineraries when it is possible. Then, they discover that living a nomadic or laptop lifestyle is not only feasible for them, but desirable. Often, they will slowly transition to traveling and working all the time. In the next chapter, we will look at those people who have decided to explore a nomadic lifestyle and some of the important considerations in preparing to do so.

3

Assessing Your Skills and Interests

Assessing your skills and interests is a crucial step in crafting a fulfilling nomadic professional life. Identifying what you are good at and what you enjoy can help in selecting the right opportunities and setting achievable career goals. Start by reflecting on your past experiences and accomplishments—consider the tasks and projects you excelled in and felt passionate about. Utilize tools like self-assessment tests and career quizzes to gain further insights into your abilities and preferences.

Engage in conversations with peers, mentors, and industry professionals to get feedback and different perspectives on your strengths and areas for improvement. Research your interests on the internet and YouTube for careers that might be interesting, fulfilling, and lucrative. Finally, keep a journal to record your thoughts and track any patterns that emerge over time. Understanding your unique skill set and interests will empower you to make informed decisions and navigate your professional journey with confidence.

The surge in remote work has opened up a plethora of opportunities in various fields, allowing professionals to work from virtually anywhere with an internet connection. Here are some popular remote job options to consider:

1. **Freelance Writing and Content Creation:** If you have a knack for words and storytelling, freelance writing offers flexibility and a variety of assignments, from blog posts and articles to copy writing and script writing.

2. **Graphic Design and Multimedia Art:** Creatives who flourish in visual communication can find remote opportunities in designing websites, marketing materials, and multimedia content for diverse industries.

3. **Software Development and Programming:** With high demand in the tech industry, software developers can work remotely, engaging in tasks such as coding, application development, and system management.

4. **Digital Marketing and Social Media Management:** Businesses increasingly rely on online presence and engagement, creating a demand for professionals skilled in SEO, content strategy, and social media marketing. Create your own *Digital Marketing Agency*.

5. **Virtual Assistance and Customer Support:** These roles provide administrative support from afar, performing tasks like managing schedules, handling customer inquiries, and performing data entry.

6. **Online Tutoring and Education:** With the rise of e-learning, educators and tutors can teach subjects, offer coaching, or create educational content from the comfort of their own homes.

7. **Data Analysis and Market Research:** Analysts mine and interpret data to help businesses make informed decisions, a role well-suited for remote work given the nature of data processing and reporting.

8. **Remote Project Management:** Coordinators who excel in organization and communication can oversee projects, manage teams, and ensure timely delivery of objectives without being physically present.

9. **YouTube Content Creator:** Suited to individuals who enjoy creating video content, and learning how to earn money from their YouTube channels.

10. **Publishing/Audio Book Creator:** This can be a lucrative endeavor for those interested in publishing and taking advantage of ai writing assistants. Creating audio-books can also be another source of income closely aligned with publishing.

Adopting a nomadic lifestyle requires a thorough understanding of both your strengths and weaknesses. Recognizing your strengths can help you leverage them to build a fulfilling and successful life on the move. Key strengths beneficial to nomads include adaptability, self-discipline, and strong organizational skills. If you thrive in new environments, can effectively manage your time, and stay productive without a fixed workspace, you're likely well-suited to this lifestyle.

On the other hand, it's crucial to acknowledge your weaknesses to prepare adequately for potential challenges. Common weaknesses might include a need for stability, difficulty with self-motivation, or a tendency to feel isolated. If you struggle without a routine, find it hard to stay driven without external accountability, or feel lonely when away from a familiar community, taking steps to mitigate these weaknesses will be vital. Strategies might include setting up a consistent daily schedule, finding remote work communities, or scheduling regular check-ins with friends and family.

Understanding these aspects of yourself will help you make an informed decision about whether a nomadic lifestyle is right for you and how to best prepare for its unique demands and opportunities if you decide to go ahead with the adventure.

4

The Excitement of Being a Digital Nomad

T he allure of the digital nomad lifestyle lies in its promise of freedom and adventure. As a digital nomad, you can work from virtually anywhere in the world, as long as you have a reliable internet connection. This flexibility allows you to explore new cultures, cuisines, and landscapes while maintaining your professional responsibilities. Imagine waking up to the sound of ocean waves in Bali or taking a break to sip coffee in a quaint café in Paris.

The world becomes your office, and each day offers a new backdrop against which you can tackle your tasks. This dynamic lifestyle not only fuels your creativity but also broadens your perspectives, providing endless opportunities for personal and professional growth.

Selecting the right destination is a crucial step in your digital nomad journey. When evaluating potential locations, consider factors such as cost of living, internet connectivity, safety, and climate. Cities like Chiang Mai, Bali, and Lisbon have become popular hubs for digital nomads due to their affordable lifestyles, vibrant communities, and excellent infrastructure. Additionally, it's wise to research visa requirements to ensure you can stay for an extended period without legal complications. Engaging with online forums and communities can provide firsthand insights and recommendations, helping you make an informed decision about your next home away from home.

Popular Destinations for Digital Nomads

1. **Bali, Indonesia**: Known for its stunning beaches, vibrant culture, and affordable cost of living, Bali tops the list for many digital nomads. The island offers a plethora of co-working spaces, lively expat communities, and an overall atmosphere conducive to work and relaxation.
2. **Chiang Mai, Thailand**: This city is a magnet for digital nomads due to its low cost of living, rich cultural heritage, and excellent internet connectivity. Chiang Mai's laid-back pace and numerous cafes and co-working spaces make it an ideal spot for remote workers.
3. **Lisbon, Portugal**: Lisbon combines old-world charm with modern amenities, making it a favorite among digital nomads. The city boasts affordable living costs, a warm climate, and a plethora of work-friendly cafes and co-working environments. Its vibrant nightlife and cultural scene are added bonuses.
4. **Medellín, Colombia**: Once infamous, Medellín has reinvented itself into a digital nomad haven. With its mild climate, affordable cost of living, and burgeoning tech scene, the city offers a refreshing blend of tradition and innovation. The welcoming local community and

increasing number of co-working spaces add to its appeal.

5. **Budapest, Hungary**: This European gem offers an intriguing mix of history, affordability, and modern infrastructure. Budapest's vibrant arts scene, efficient public transport, and numerous work spaces make it an attractive base for digital nomads. The city's rich cultural landscape ensures that there's always something new to explore.

6. **Ho Chi Minh City, Vietnam**: Ho Chi Minh City, or Saigon, is rapidly growing in popularity among digital nomads for its dynamic energy, low living costs, and excellent internet speeds. The city's bustling street life and diverse food scene make it an exciting place to live and work remotely.

7. **Prague, Czech Republic**: Known for its stunning architecture and lively social scene, Prague is an excellent destination for digital nomads. The city offers a good balance of affordable living, reliable internet connectivity, and a thriving coffee culture. Its well-preserved medieval buildings, charming cafés, and extensive public transport system make it both a practical and delightful place for remote work.

8. **Bali, Indonesia**: Bali remains a perennial favorite among digital nomads. The island's natural beauty, combined with its numerous co-working spaces and strong expatriate community, makes it ideal for those seeking a balance between productivity and leisure. Affordable living costs, tropical climate, and a laid-back lifestyle add to its allure.

9. **Barcelona, Spain**: Famed for its art, architecture, and Mediterranean lifestyle, Barcelona has much to offer digital nomads. The city features a plethora of co-working spaces, a robust public transport system, and myriad

cultural activities. Its diverse culinary scene and sunny weather make it an appealing choice for remote workers.

10. **Tbilisi, Georgia**: Tbilisi is gaining traction as an up-and-coming destination for digital nomads due to its affordability, hospitable locals, and burgeoning tech scene. The city offers an intriguing blend of ancient history and modern amenities, alongside a one-year digital nomad visa program. The local cuisine and beautiful landscapes add to its charm.

Popular Beach Communities for Digital Nomads

1. **Canggu, Bali**: Among the trendy beach communities in Bali, Canggu tops the list for digital nomads. Known for its surf-friendly beaches, vibrant café scene, and co-working spaces, Canggu offers a perfect balance between work and play. The area's relaxed vibe and numerous wellness centers make it appealing to those looking to maintain a healthy lifestyle while working remotely.

2. **Playa del Carmen, Mexico**: This Mexican beach town is renowned for its crystal-clear waters and bustling digital nomad community. Playa del Carmen features several co-working spaces and high-speed internet, making it easy to stay productive. The town's proximity to tourist attractions like cenotes, Mayan ruins, and adventure parks makes it a great spot for combining work with exploration.

3. **Lisbon, Portugal**: While not a traditional beach town, Lisbon is close to several stunning beaches like Cascais and Estoril, making it a favored spot for digital nomads

who enjoy coastal living. The city provides an excellent blend of historical charm, modern amenities, and a vibrant start-up scene. Lisbon's mild climate, affordable cost of living, and delicious food further enhance its appeal.

4. **Chiang Mai, Thailand**: Although primarily known as a mountainous city, Chiang Mai has easy flight access to some of Thailand's most beautiful beaches, such as Koh Samui and Phuket. Chiang Mai's extensive digital nomad community, affordable living, and serene environment make it a temporary home for many remote workers who also want to explore Thailand's coastal paradises during weekends and holidays.

5. **Santa Teresa, Costa Rica**: This laid-back beach town is a burgeoning hotspot for digital nomads seeking a blend of remote work and surf culture. With its beautiful beaches, reliable internet, and growing number of co-working spaces, Santa Teresa provides a point of tranquility and productivity. The surrounding jungle and local wildlife add a unique touch, making it an ideal destination for nature lovers.

These destinations are just the tip of the iceberg, and each offers a unique experience for digital nomads. Whether you're seeking serene nature, historical richness, or a bustling city atmosphere, there's a place out there that can perfectly match your work and lifestyle preferences.

Personal Growth

Embarking on the digital nomad journey offers numerous opportunities for personal growth. One of the most profound areas of development is self-reliance. Navigating new cities, managing logistics, and handling unexpected challenges on your own fosters a sense of independence and confidence. Additionally, digital nomads often become more culturally aware and open-minded, as they are exposed to diverse customs, languages, and perspectives. This increased cultural sensitivity can lead to improved communication skills and a deeper appreciation for global diversity.

Living a life on the move also cultivates adaptability and resilience. Constantly changing environments require digital nomads to be flexible and resourceful, quickly adjusting to new situations and making decisions on the fly. Moreover, with the absence of a traditional work structure, digital nomads often develop better time management skills, learning how to prioritize tasks and maintain productivity amidst distractions.

Furthermore, the experience of being a digital nomad can enhance one's problem-solving abilities and creativity. Facing new challenges and environments regularly encourages innovative thinking and the ability to find novel solutions. Lastly, many digital nomads report a heightened sense of purpose and fulfillment as they align their work with their passion for travel and exploration, creating a balanced and enriching lifestyle.

In summary, the digital nomad lifestyle offers not only professional opportunities but also personal growth and development. By immersing oneself in new cultures, being self-reliant, adaptable, and creative, digital nomads can expand their skill set and mindset while living a fulfilling and enriching life on the road. So, it is essential to embrace the challenges and opportunities for personal as well as professional growth.

The importance of planning.

Planning and organizational skills are critical to your success. Without a structured approach, managing work tasks, travel logistics, and personal time can become overwhelming. It is crucial to develop a well-thought-out plan that includes not only a work schedule but also a financial plan and a strategy for staying connected with clients or employers. Additionally, organizing travel documents, setting up reliable internet access, and identifying suitable workspace in advance can prevent disruptions and ensure productivity.

Write it down. Commit your planning and organization to either a planning notebook or to a software program that allows you to plan meticulously to keep track of your decisions and activities. Take the time to prioritize your responsibilities and tasks in your professional life, as well as your personal life. Plan these separately, so that when your professional tasks are finished, you can then flip the page, and embrace the activities you want to pursue in your travels.

By prioritizing planning and organization, digital nomads can create a stable foundation that allows them to thrive both professionally and personally, regardless of where their journeys take them. So if you are interested in embarking on a digital nomad lifestyle, take the time to carefully plan and prepare. With determination and adaptability, you can enjoy the freedom, flexibility, and personal growth that comes with being a digital nomad. Whether you choose to travel to different countries or simply work remotely from your own hometown, this unique lifestyle offers endless opportunities for discovery, adventure, and growth. With the right mindset, skills, and tools, you can successfully navigate the challenges and reap the rewards of being a digital nomad.

Continue learning new skills, staying organized, and prioritizing self-care to make the most out of this lifestyle. Connect with other digital nomads for support and inspiration, and remember to always stay open-minded and adaptable as the world of remote work continues to evolve. Join online forums and groups, attend meetups and conferences, and connect with other digital nomads through social media.

Not only can this help you build a support system for when you're on the road, but it also allows you to make valuable connections and potentially collaborate with other nomads on projects. You can collaborate with other travelers about endless questions you may have. For example, the best places to stay in Asia, what equipment to use for your job, and even how to find new cuisine in an unknown city. Additionally, staying connected can provide you with inspiration and ideas for new destinations, remote work opportunities, and ways to improve your digital nomad lifestyle.

The possibilities are endless when it comes to being a digital nomad, so keep an open mind and be willing to adapt to new experiences and challenges along the way. With determination, passion, and a love for exploration, you can thrive as a digital nomad and create a fulfilling and meaningful life on your own terms. So start planning, pack your bags, and get ready to embark on an exciting journey of work, travel, and personal growth as a digital nomad! Keep exploring, learning, and embracing new opportunities – the world is your office and there's always something new to discover.

5

Prioritize Self-Care

I t's important to prioritize self-care as a digital nomad. With the freedom to work from anywhere comes the responsibility to take care of yourself.

Becoming a digital nomad requires a significant mindset and lifestyle shift. It's essential to let go of traditional notions of work, such as the 9-5 office routine or job security, and embrace a flexible, location-independent approach to your career. This transition can also bring about a change in daily routines, such as adjusting to different time zones and finding new ways to stay motivated and focused while working in ever-changing environments. Embracing a minimalist lifestyle, both physically and mentally, can also be beneficial for digital nomads as it allows for easier travel and reduces distractions from work. Additionally, being open-minded and adaptable to change is crucial as unexpected challenges may arise while on the road. Don't hesitate to reach out to family, friends, or professional counselors if you feel overwhelmed. Sometimes, simply talking about your challenges can provide relief and new perspectives.

Self-Care Specifics

This includes physically, mentally, and emotionally. Ensure that you maintain a balanced routine that includes regular exercise, healthy eating, and adequate sleep. This might mean finding local gyms, exploring outdoor activities, or preparing your own meals to avoid the temptations of fast food. Mental health is equally important, so incorporate practices like meditation, journaling, or even seeking virtual therapy sessions if needed.

Journaling about your experiences with your work life and personal life on the road is highly recommended. This is a way to build self-reflection into your decisions, and to adjust to your circumstances. Writing in a journal is a powerful way to stay grounded and maintaining stability in your new environments. However, don't let it take the place of communicating with others, which is just as important to your mental health.

Moreover, setting clear boundaries between your work and personal life is essential to avoid burnout. Establish dedicated work hours and find suitable work spaces that allow you to focus without distractions. This approach helps maintain productivity while giving you the time to enjoy the new and exciting places you visit.

Strategies for Maintaining Work-Life Balance

Achieving a healthy work-life balance is essential for long-term well-being and productivity while being a digital nomad. These are very helpful in providing a sense of stability and purpose. Here are some strategies to help you maintain that balance:

1. **Set Clear Boundaries**: Define specific work hours and stick to them. Communicate these boundaries to your colleagues, family, and friends, ensuring everyone understands when you are available for work and when you are not. Despite living in a foreign country, digital communication tools can be used to interrupt you during work hours wherever you are, so let others know when you will be working.

2. **Prioritize and Delegate Tasks**: Identify your most important tasks and focus on completing them first. Don't hesitate to delegate tasks that others can handle to free up your time for more critical responsibilities.

3. **Take Regular Breaks**: Short breaks throughout the day can help you recharge and maintain focus. Use techniques like the Pomodoro Technique, which involves working for 25 minutes and then taking a 5-minute break. Plan for meals-this is essential. Your health is your priority, so do not skip meals.

4. **Create a Dedicated Workspace**: Having a specific area in your living space designated for work can help you mentally separate your professional and personal life. Avoid working in areas meant for relaxation.

5. **Unplug After Work**: Once your workday is over, make a conscious effort to disconnect from work-related devices

and emails. This time should be reserved for personal activities, hobbies, and spending time on your travel goals.

6. **Set Personal Goals**: Just as you set professional goals, establish personal goals that matter to you. Whether it's reading a book, learning a new skill, or spending more time establishing a social network, having clear personal objectives can help you maintain balance.

7. **Practice Self-Care**: Regular exercise, healthy eating, and sufficient sleep are crucial for maintaining energy levels and focus. Incorporating mindfulness practices, such as meditation or yoga, can also enhance your mental well-being.

8. **Seek Support**: Reach out for help if you need it. All of us need help at one time or another. Don't deprive yourself of this basic human need.

Finally, embrace the unpredictability of the digital nomad lifestyle. Flexibility and adaptability are key traits of successful digital nomads. Challenges such as changing time zones, unreliable internet connections, or unexpected travel hurdles are part of the journey. Learning to navigate these issues with a positive attitude and a problem-solving mindset will make your digital nomad experience far more rewarding. Remember, the essence of being a digital nomad is not just about working remotely; it's about creating a life filled with rich experiences, continuous learning, and personal growth.

In addition to prioritizing self-care, it's also important for digital nomads to prioritize their finances. With a lifestyle that involves frequent travel and potentially unstable income, it's crucial to have a solid financial plan in place.

First and foremost, keep track of your expenses and create a budget that works for your individual situation. Again, make sure you put your budget in writing. You will want to balance your income with expenses. Be very rational when assessing your budget. You do not want to run out of money while you are traveling. A written budget will help you stay on top of your finances and make necessary adjustments when needed. It is good to remember that budgets are not written in stone. As income and expenses change, adjust your budget accordingly.

It's also wise to have multiple streams of income as a digital nomad. Don't rely solely on one client or source of income; diversify your skills and services to increase your potential earnings. This can include freelance work, creating passive income streams, or even starting your own online business.

Additionally, research and take advantage of cost-saving opportunities while traveling. This can include using travel rewards credit cards, finding affordable accommodations through home-sharing platforms, or even negotiating lower prices for long-term stays.

Finally, it's important to plan for the future and have a safety net in case of emergencies. Consider investing in retirement savings or emergency funds to provide financial stability in the long run.

Another aspect of planning is to have a Plan B if your nomadic lifestyle becomes too difficult to support. Plan for what you will do if you get low on money. If you have to pack up and leave whatever country you are living in, have a back-up living situation lined up so that you have a safe place to return to where you are welcome and have support. This could be trusted friends or family members. But, this is an essential step to your success as a digital nomad, so you can set your Plan A into motion with confidence.

So with this in mind, by prioritizing self-care and managing your finances, you can create a sustainable and fulfilling digital nomad lifestyle. With a problem-solving mindset and strategic planning, you can navigate any challenges that may arise and continue to thrive as a digital nomad. Keep learning, stay open-minded, and enjoy the journey!

6

Navigating Different Cultures

One of the most exciting aspects of being a nomadic professional is getting to experience different cultures and ways of life. However, it's important to be aware of cultural differences and norms in order to avoid unintentionally causing offense or misunderstanding. Doing some research before traveling to a new destination can help you navigate these differences with respect and sensitivity. Additionally, being open-minded and adaptable can go a long way in making the most of your travel experiences.

Embracing cultural diversity can enrich your journey and broaden your perspective. As you travel to various places, take time to learn about local customs, traditions, and social etiquette. This might include understanding dining customs, dress codes, or social greetings that are customary in different cultures. For example, in some Asian countries, removing your shoes before entering a home is a sign of respect, while in many European cultures, a firm handshake is a standard form of greeting.

Learning a few key phrases in the local language can also make a significant difference in your interactions, showing respect and willingness to engage with local people. Additionally, try to be mindful of non-verbal communication, as gestures and body language can vary significantly from one culture to another.

Approaching each new culture with curiosity and humility will not only help you form meaningful connections but also enhance your understanding and appreciation of the world's rich tapestry of human experience. Remember, cultural navigation is not just about avoiding faux pas; it's about building bridges and fostering mutual respect and understanding.

Some digital nomads report that learning to live within another culture has been the most important part of their work and travel experience. Some have developed friendships that have lasted decades. Others have met their spouses while living abroad. And others have learned to be tremendously grateful for the lives they have been able to live.

English is often understood and spoken in many foreign countries which helps facilitate communication. In addition there are apps on smart phones and different devices you can purchase that will translate different languages in real time. Even thought it is possible to communicate, it is important to understand that being able to communicate about daily activities does not necessarily mean that you understand all the nuances that a specific culture brings to a situation. Don't make assumptions that you know how another person feels in the country where you are visiting. By doing this, you can keep your communication respectful and positive.

7

The Low Budget Nomad

One effective way to manage a low budget for technical items as a digital nomad is to prioritize versatile and multi-functional devices. For instance, opting for a high-quality laptop that can handle a variety of tasks efficiently can eliminate the need for additional gadgets. Look for refurbished or second-hand options, which can offer substantial savings compared to brand-new models. Additionally, consider utilizing cloud-based services to minimize the need for expensive storage solutions.

Platforms like Google Drive, Dropbox, and OneDrive provide ample storage at a fraction of the cost of physical hard drives. Exploring community-driven platforms and digital nomad groups (Facebook groups) can also yield recommendations for cost-saving tools and technologies. Often, fellow nomads will share valuable insights on where to find discounts or deals on essential gear as well as other tips to reduce expenses. Finally, remember to take advantage of free software and open-source solutions that can perform many of the same functions as paid alternatives, enabling you to complete your work efficiently without breaking the bank.

Reducing expenses requires a strategic approach to both your lifestyle and your work habits. Firstly, consider leveraging house-sitting opportunities or staying in co-living spaces, which can be more cost-effective than traditional accommodation arrangements like hotels or short-term rentals. Websites like TrustedHousesitters and NomadX offer platforms where you can find such opportunities.

Another practical tip is to embrace slow travel. By spending longer periods in fewer destinations, you can benefit from lower accommodation rates and reduced transportation costs. Additionally, choosing destinations with a lower cost of living can significantly stretch your budget. Many digital nomads find that countries in Southeast Asia, Eastern Europe, and South America offer an affordable yet enriching experience. On the work front, utilizing free and open-source software can also lead to substantial savings. Tools like GIMP for image editing, LibreOffice for productivity, and KanbanFlow for task management provide robust functionalities without the hefty price tags of their commercial counterparts.

Don't forget to consistently review and cancel subscriptions to services and tools you no longer use or need. Lastly, indulge in local cuisine. Eating at local markets and street vendors rather than international chain restaurants not only reduces meal costs but also offers a more authentic culinary experience. By adopting these cost-cutting strategies, digital nomads can maintain financial health while fully enjoying their nomadic journey.

8

Conclusion

As with any lifestyle change, there are many ways to go about it. Depending on your personality and past experiences, you may want to adjust your approach to becoming a digital nomad so you can stack the deck in your favor. This is more than an adventure we are talking about. Preparation is key to your success. If you have already traveled a lot and are familiar with travel arrangements and safety precautions, then you will be able to adapt to a nomadic lifestyle much easier than someone who has limited travel experience.

Before hopping on a plane to one of your favorite destinations, a measured approach may be the wisest. Take it a step at a time. Getting your work plans under your belt first before traveling and working can be very helpful. Establish a home office first and start working remotely just as you would if you were traveling. Once you are settled into a routine as suggested in this book, then start to take a relatively short trip, even in the same country you live in. Go with a friend at first if possible. The idea is to learn as much as you can before stepping out to the next phase of your plans. Build up your confidence. Get your technology set up on these trips. Eventually, you will be ready to travel overseas and combine your work with more extensive travel.

Plan, plan, and review your plans. Try to talk to others who have traveled to the destination you have in mind. The more you can familiarize yourself with your destination, the better off you will be. Network with other digital nomads online and ask them questions. Know all of the cultural expectations of where you are going to be staying. Make sure you will be staying in an area that is safe.

As you keep expanding your comfort zone, eventually you will be all set up in the country and situation that you want. Keep to your routine as much as possible, plan for emergencies, and enjoy your personal time! When you have accomplished your digital nomad goals, both personal and professionally, you will look back and realize that you have become a much more confident, self-reliant, and independent person!

Lastly, Develop a sense of humor: Life as a digital nomad is filled with uncertainties and unexpected challenges. Developing a sense of humor can be invaluable in navigating these ups and downs. Whether it's a missed flight, a language barrier mishap, or an unreliable internet connection, being able to laugh at the situation can reduce stress and make troubleshooting feel less daunting. Humor also bridges cultural gaps, enabling you to connect more deeply with locals and other travelers. Embracing the lighter side of nomadic life can turn frustrating moments into memorable stories and make the journey more enjoyable overall.

Remember!

"Choose a job that you like, and you will never have to work a day in your life." – *Confucius*

II

Part Two

It is suggested that you create and either print out or keep specific worksheets on your computer to keep yourself organized. Use Chatgpt or other ai generators to create these sheets. You will find a list of these sheets in Chapter 9.

9

Chapter 9

A book about being a digital nomad would not be complete without suggested worksheets. The following worksheets can provide you with practical tools for you to navigate your journey effectively. Here are some types of worksheets that should be included:

Travel Planning: These worksheets can help readers plan out their trips, including details like destination research, accommodation options, transportation plans, and crucial contacts.

Budget Management: Worksheets dedicated to budgeting can assist in tracking expenses, estimating monthly costs, and managing funds while on the move.

Time Management: Given the nature of remote work, time management is crucial. Worksheets for scheduling work hours, setting deadlines, and organizing daily tasks can be incredibly useful.

Skill Development: Readers can benefit from worksheets that focus on developing essential skills such as adaptability, self-motivation, and problem-solving.

Career Planning: Worksheets that help map out career goals, identify remote job opportunities, and network within the digital nomad community can be invaluable.

Health and Wellness: Including worksheets to track fitness routines, diet plans, and mental health practices can help maintain a balanced lifestyle.

Emergency Planning: Worksheets that outline emergency contacts, medical facilities, and contingency plans for travel disruptions can provide peace of mind.